# DIM SUM

# DIM SUM

Dumplings, parcels and other delectable
Chinese snacks in 25 authentic recipes

TERRY TAN

LORENZ BOOKS

This edition is published by
Lorenz Books, an imprint of
Anness Publishing Limited
info@anness.com
www.lorenzbooks.com
www.annesspublishing.com

If you like the images in this book
and would like to investigate using
them for publishing, promotions or
advertising, please visit our website
www.practicalpictures.com for
more information.

Publisher: Joanna Lorenz
Editor: Kate Eddison
Photographer: Martin Brigdale
Food Stylists: Katie Giovanni and
    Lucy McKelvie
Prop Stylists: Martin Brigdale and
    Helen Trent
Designer: Lisa Tai
Production Controller: Ben Worley

Front cover image shows Pork and
Cabbage Dumplings – for recipe, see
page 50.

## PUBLISHER'S NOTE

Although the advice and information in this book are believed to be accurate and true
at the time of going to press, neither the authors nor the publisher can accept any legal
responsibility or liability for any errors or omissions that may have been made nor for
any inaccuracies nor for any loss, harm or injury that comes about from following
instructions or advice in this book.

## NOTES

- Bracketed terms are intended for American readers.
- For all recipes, quantities are given in both metric and imperial measures and, where
  appropriate, in standard cups and spoons. Follow one set of measures, but not a
  mixture, because they are not interchangeable.
- Standard spoon and cup measures are level. 1 tsp = 5ml,1 tbsp = 15ml,
  1 cup = 250ml/8fl oz.
- Australian standard tablespoons are 20ml. Australian readers should use 3 tsp in
  place of 1 tbsp for measuring small quantities.
- American pints are 16fl oz/2 cups. American readers should use 20fl oz/2.5 cups in
  place of 1 pint when measuring liquids.
- Electric oven temperatures in this book are for conventional ovens. When using a fan
  oven, the temperature will probably need to be reduced by about 10–20°C/20–40°F.
  Since ovens vary, you should check with your manufacturer's instruction book
  for guidance.
- The nutritional analysis given for each recipe is calculated per portion (i.e. serving
  or item), unless otherwise stated. If the recipe gives a range, such as Serves 4–6,
  then the nutritional analysis will be for the smaller portion size, i.e. 6 servings.
  The analysis does not include optional ingredients, such as salt added to taste.
- Medium (US large) eggs are used unless otherwise stated.

# Contents

# 'Food to Touch the Heart'

Dim sum, which translates as 'food to touch the heart' is immensely popular throughout China and the rest of the world. Dim sum is traditionally a Cantonese way of eating, and its ancient beginnings in Guangdong are linked to the Chinese penchant for consuming light snacks with tea.

### WHAT IS DIM SUM?

Dim sum were never meant to provide a full meal, and favourites such as cha siew bau (Roast Pork Dumplings), shao mai (Minced Pork Dumplings) and xiao long bau (Little Dragon Dumplings) were originally served much like Spanish tapas – as a light snack.

Over time, however, the range has grown and today eating dim sum invariably means consuming an eclectic variety of small dishes that can comprise a full meal. Dim sum restaurants sprang up to meet the growing demand for this type of dining, and are now the venue of choice worldwide.

### REGIONAL VARIATIONS

Dim sum is now enjoyed all over China. Every region makes use of indigenous ingredients, meaning that each province has its own dim sum menu, as well as sharing some

Below: *Bamboo steamers come in a variety of sizes.*

Above: *Only a few tools are needed to make dim sum at home.*

Above: *A mortar and pestle can be used to mince (grind) soft shellfish.*

Above: *A selection of tiny dipping bowls is essential for authentic presentation.*

national classics. Fried or steamed, wrapped with rice or wheat flour batters, there is a growing list of new types of dim sum joining the tried-and-tested repertoire. Seasonings and dips, on the other hand, remain within the traditional Cantonese canon of black bean sauce, hoisin sauce, sesame oil, garlic and spring onions (scallions).

## EQUIPMENT

The traditional Chinese kitchen is quite basic, often consisting of an open hearth and simple implements such as woks, cleavers and steamers. The wok is the most

important piece of equipment in every Chinese kitchen, and it is essential for making dim sum. Woks are used for stir-frying dim sum fillings, as well as for steaming and deep-frying the morsels.

A cleaver is useful for chopping ingredients finely, but a heavy knife can be used instead. A mortar and pestle are also handy for mixing dumpling fillings, as they retain a much better texture than using a food processor.

Bamboo steamers are inexpensive and come in many sizes. They have porous lids that do not trap steam inside. Today,

aluminium steamers are also available. Multiple stack steamers are useful for cooking many dishes at once.

For deep-fried dim sum, you will need a slotted spoon to retrieve the food from the hot oil, and some kitchen paper on which to drain the cooked items.

Chopsticks should be provided for diners, and small Chinese dipping bowls are a pleasing way to complete the authentic presentation. A selection of little bowls is always useful, as you will often want to serve more than one dipping sauce, to cater for different tastes.

Above: *Beancurd skins are commonly used as dim sum wrappers.*

Above: *Wonton wrappers are a good choice for deep-fried bites.*

Above: *Black vinegar provides deep flavour in various dipping sauces.*

## FILLING INGREDIENTS

Dim sum are made with a vast range of oriental ingredients, most of which can now be bought outside of China. The inclusion of exotic vegetables such as mooli (daikon), jicama, taro, bamboo shoots and Chinese chives create the tastes and textures of authentic Chinese cuisine. If they are not readily available in your local supermarket, try shopping in Chinese stores. Prawns (shrimp) are one of the most popular dumpling fillings, along with minced (ground) pork, chicken and, occasionally, beef.

## WRAPPERS

A wide variety of wrappers can be purchased, which allows you to prepare dim sum quickly and easily at home. Wonton wrappers, beancurd skins and Chinese wafer pastry are used to delicious effect in this book.

## MAKING DIM SUM DOUGH

There is no single recipe for dim sum dough, as chefs across the country have developed their own recipes using available ingredients. Doughs are commonly made with a combination of the following: wheat starch, cornflour

(cornstarch), sweet potato flour, tapioca flour, glutinous rice flour, high-gluten flour (gou garn fun), low-gluten flour (dai garn fun), plain (all-purpose) flour or even self-raising (self-rising) flour. Whatever the principal ingredient, dim sum doughs are always delicate and often translucent when cooked.

## DIPPING SAUCES

Some recipes have a specific dip to accompany them, and recipes for these are provided where necessary. However, most dim sum will be delicious served with store-bought sauces such as soy sauce, black vinegar, chilli sauce or chilli oil, which are all available in Chinese stores. Serve a selection for diners to mix and match.

## DIM SUM TODAY
As a meal for one or ten, the most appealing element of modern dim sum is the wonderful variety. In dim sum restaurants, the diners are free to eat what they like from the dim sum trolley, and are not dictated to by a rigid menu. Chefs from all over China have been challenged to be ever more inventive in preparing bitesize morsels, dumplings, snacks and assorted finger food, using combinations of vegetables, tofu, fish, shellfish, poultry and meat.

At home, cooks are likely to choose one or two dishes, perhaps as an appetizer or party snack. However, with some preparation and the right equipment, the adventurous home cook can also whip up a medley of delights to create their own dim sum meal. Opt for a variety of fillings, both fried and steamed.

## TEA
Dim sum is inextricably linked to drinking tea. Cantonese tea houses are the home of dim sum, and a multitude of teas are served. Although there are hundreds of varieties of tea, they all fall into two basic categories, black (sometimes called red) and green. Both types come from the same plant and the chief differences lie in processing. Black tea is first fermented, or oxidized, which is the technical term for this process. When it is only semi-fermented, or semi-oxidized, it is called Oolong tea. The name is derived from Wu Long, meaning 'black dragon', and the strongest of these is Tie Guan Yin, meaning 'iron goddess of mercy'. Green tea is unfermented and is dried in the sun or in special drying kilns, where the leaves may also be steamed to make them soft. They are then rolled and fired in the kilns until they turn a yellowish-green and take on their unique curled shape. The finest teas are still hand-processed, especially the rare teas such as Gunpowder and Dragon Well.

# Yam Cake

The vegetable on which this Cantonese classic is based inevitably causes confusion. In America, where yam can refer to an orange-fleshed sweet potato, this vegetable is called taro. What you need here is the large barrel-shaped vegetable with a hairy brown skin and purple-flecked flesh.

**SERVES 6–8**

50g/2oz dried shrimp
75ml/5 tbsp vegetable oil
15 shallots, thinly sliced
2 Chinese sausages, diced finely
1kg/2¼lb yam (taro)
300g/11oz/2 cups rice flour
115g/4oz/1 cup tapioca flour or
  cornflour (cornstarch)
750ml/1¼ pints/2 cups water
5ml/1 tsp salt
2 spring onions (scallions), plus
  extra, chopped, to garnish
30ml/2 tbsp light soy sauce
30ml/2 tbsp sesame oil
2.5ml/½ tsp ground black pepper
chilli dipping sauce, for serving

1  Put the dried shrimp in a bowl and pour over water to cover. Soak for 1 hour, until soft. Heat the oil in a frying pan and fry the shallots for 4–5 minutes, until brown and crisp. Lift out with a slotted spoon and set aside.

2  Drain the soaked shrimp and chop them roughly. Reheat the oil remaining in the pan and fry the shrimp with the diced sausage for 3 minutes. Transfer the shrimp and sausage to a bowl and set aside.

3  Peel the yam and remove the fibrous stalk. Cut the flesh into large chunks, then steam over simmering water for 20 minutes until the flesh is soft.

4  Put the yam into a large bowl and mash with a potato masher. Stir in the rice flour and the tapioca or cornflour, then add the water and salt. Mix well.

5  Set aside 30ml/2 tbsp of the fried shallots. Add the remainder to the shrimp mixture. Stir in the spring onions, soy sauce, sesame oil and pepper. Fry gently in a hot wok for 2 minutes so that the flavours combine.

6  Add the mixture to the mashed yams. Mix well, then press into a lightly oiled steaming tray. Sprinkle half the reserved fried shallots over the surface. Steam over rapidly boiling water for 15 minutes.

7  Allow to cool, then cut into wedges. Garnish with the rest of the fried shallots and some chopped spring onions, and serve with the chilli dipping sauce.

**COOK'S TIP**
Dried shrimp are sold in most Chinese food stores. They have a very strong smell, but this dissipates when they are cooked.

Per portion Energy 481kcal/2025kJ; Protein 9.9g; Carbohydrate 79.6g, of which sugars 2.6g; Fat 14.6g, of which saturates 2.9g; Cholesterol 37mg; Calcium 121mg; Fibre 3g; Sodium 648mg.

# Radish Cake

Closely related to yam cake, this recipe makes innovative use of the large white radish that is also known as mooli or daikon. As a vegetable, white radish is fairly bland, although it is useful for making soup stock. Process it to a paste and mix it with rice flour, however, and it is magically transformed.

## SERVES 6–8

50g/2oz dried shrimp
1kg/2¼lb mooli (daikon) or
  'white radish'
300g/11oz/2 cups rice flour
115g/4oz/1 cup tapioca flour or
  cornflour (cornstarch)
750ml/1¼ pints/3 cups water
5ml/1 tsp salt
30ml/2 tbsp vegetable oil
30ml/2 tbsp light soy sauce
30ml/2 tbsp sesame oil
2.5ml/½ tsp ground black pepper
soy sauce and chopped chillies,
  to serve

### COOK'S TIPS
• White radishes are much larger than the more common red variety and can weigh up to 1kg/2¼lb. Choose ones that are pearly white and firm, as old radishes become fibrous.
• Radish cake can be frozen and thawed without losing any of its flavour.

1 Put the dried shrimp in a bowl and pour over enough water to cover. Soak for 1 hour, until soft.

2 Meanwhile, peel the mooli and chop it roughly. Process the mooli, in batches, in a blender or food processor to a soft white purée. Scrape the mooli into a sieve (strainer) and press down with a spoon to extract as much liquid as possible.

3 Tip the mooli purée into a bowl and stir in the rice flour and the tapioca or cornflour. Add the water and salt. Mix well.

4 Drain the soaked shrimp and chop them roughly.

5 Spoon the mooli purée into a non-stick pan and cook over low heat, stirring frequently, for 5 minutes.

6 Heat the vegetable oil in a frying pan or wok. Add the chopped shrimp and fry for 2 minutes, then add the mooli purée. Stir well, then add the soy sauce, sesame oil and black pepper. Mix thoroughly to combine.

7 Press the mixture into a lightly oiled steaming tray. Steam over a pan or wok of rapidly boiling water for 20 minutes. Set aside to cool completely.

8 When cold, slice into bite-size pieces and serve plain or with a dipping sauce of soy sauce mixed with chopped chillies.

Per portion Energy 263kcal/1099kJ; Protein 7g; Carbohydrate 44.2g, of which sugars 2.7g; Fat 6.3g, of which saturates 0.9g; Cholesterol 32mg; Calcium 111mg; Fibre 1.9g; Sodium 560mg.

# Pumpkin Cake

This delicious Fujian snack is often made during festive occasions. It is one of the most comforting foods on the eastern Chinese menu and a lovely way to use up pumpkin when all the Halloween madness is over. This is a savoury-yet-sweet concoction that is usually served at Chinese New Year.

### SERVES 6–8

1kg/2¼lb pumpkin, cut into
    even chunks
300g/11oz/2⅔ cups rice flour
30ml/2 tbsp tapioca flour
50g/2oz dried shrimps, soaked
    for 1 hour, and drained
8 Chinese dried mushrooms,
    soaked until soft
45ml/3 tbsp vegetable oil
4 garlic cloves, crushed
1 Chinese sausage, cut into
    very small dice
15ml/1 tbsp sesame oil
30ml/2 tbsp light soy sauce
2.5ml/½ tsp ground white pepper
sliced cucumber and soy sauce,
    to serve

### COOK'S TIP
This is very similar to the famous Yam Cake of South China (page 10), but it needs to steam for longer.

1   Steam the pumpkin for 20 minutes, or until soft enough to mash easily. Allow the pumpkin to cool, then process it to a fine paste using a food processor or potato masher.

2   Mix the rice flour, tapioca flour and mashed pumpkin together. Stir to mix thoroughly until the mixture is a smooth paste with the consistency of thick batter.

3   Chop the soaked dried shrimps roughly. Snip off and discard the stems of the soaked mushrooms, then slice the caps.

4   Heat the oil in a wok and fry the garlic for 30 seconds until light brown. Add the dried shrimps, mushrooms and sausage, and fry for 1 minute. Add the sesame oil, soy sauce and pepper, and stir for 30 seconds until well mixed.

5   Mix well with the prepared pumpkin mash, making sure the ingredients are well distributed.

6   Transfer to a lightly oiled steaming tray and press gently with a spatula to form a firm, round cake. Steam for 25 minutes or until cooked through, then allow to cool completely.

7   Once cool, chill the cake until ready to serve. Cut into wedges and serve with cucumber slices and soy sauce for dipping.

Per portion Energy 267kcal/1115kJ; Protein 8g; Carbohydrate 40g, of which sugars 2g; Fat 8g, of which saturates 1g; Cholesterol 32mg; Calcium 126g; Fibre 1g; Sodium 542mg.

# Crystal Dumplings

A much-loved street food, these dumplings are often sold by vendors carrying their wares in two baskets slung either side of a long bamboo pole. They are called chui kuay (water dumplings) by the Swatow-speaking Shantou people on account of their translucent skins.

## SERVES 6–8

200g/7oz/1¾ cups sweet
  potato flour
400ml/14fl oz/1⅔ cups water
30ml/2 tbsp vegetable oil
115g/4oz/1 cup tapioca flour

### For the filling
400g/14oz can bamboo
  shoots, drained
45ml/3 tbsp vegetable oil
3 garlic cloves, crushed
30ml/2 tbsp dark soy sauce
30ml/2 tbsp oyster sauce
5ml/1 tsp ground black pepper
200ml/7fl oz/scant 1 cup water

### For the soy sauce and chilli dip
45ml/3 tbsp dark soy sauce
15ml/1 tbsp ginger purée
15ml/1 tbsp rice vinegar
15ml/1 tbsp sesame oil
5ml/1 tsp sugar
5ml/1 tsp chilli bean paste

1  Put the sweet potato flour in a non-stick pan. Add the water and oil, and cook over low heat, stirring occasionally, until thick. Leave to cool for 15 minutes.

2  Meanwhile, shred the bamboo shoots for the filling until they are the shape and size of beansprouts. Put them in a colander, rinse thoroughly and drain.

3  Heat the oil in a wok and fry the garlic over low heat for 40 seconds. Do not let it burn. Add the bamboo shoots, soy sauce, oyster sauce, pepper and water. Cook over medium heat for 10 minutes, until the mixture is almost dry. Leave to cool.

4  Stir the tapioca flour into the cool sweet potato flour mixture. Mix well, then transfer to a floured board. Knead for at least 5 minutes, punching the dough as you work. Shape the dough into a long roll, about 5cm/2in in diameter. Slice off pieces 9mm/⅜in thick and flatten each with a rolling pin to form very thin circles.

5  Place 30ml/2 tbsp of the bamboo shoot mixture on each dough circle, fold over into a half-moon shape and seal the edges. Trim off any excess dough and fold and pinch until you get a serrated edge on each dumpling. Place the dumplings on a lightly oiled plate and steam over rapidly boiling water for 30 minutes, topping up the water as necessary.

6  Meanwhile, mix together all the ingredients for the dip, and transfer to a serving bowl. Serve the dumplings warm with the dip.

Per portion Energy 244kcal/1022kJ; Protein 3.6g; Carbohydrate 38.2g, of which sugars 5.2g; Fat 8.7g, of which saturates 1.1g; Cholesterol 0mg; Calcium 21mg; Fibre 1.3g; Sodium 1134mg.

# Jicama Dumplings

The filling for these dumplings is made with jicama, a root vegetable that resembles a large, sweet turnip with a thin brown skin. It tastes faintly of crunchy water chestnuts and goes well with prawns and soy sauce in these light, steamed dim sum.

**SERVES 4**

75g/3oz wheat starch or glutinous rice flour, plus extra for dusting
90g/3½oz/generous ⅔ cup cornflour (cornstarch)
about 250ml/8fl oz/1 cup boiling water
15ml/1 tbsp vegetable oil
sweet soy sauce (kicap manis), to serve

### For the filling

250g/9oz jicama, peeled and thinly sliced into rounds
25g/1oz/2 tbsp dried shrimp, soaked for 15 minutes
45ml/3 tbsp groundnut (peanut) oil
2 garlic cloves, crushed
30ml/2 tbsp light soy sauce
5ml/1 tsp ground black pepper

1 To make the filling, slice the jicama rounds into thin strips, then wash and drain well. Drain the soaked shrimp, and crush them with a mortar and pestle.
2 Heat the oil in a wok or heavy pan and fry the garlic for 30 seconds. Add the jicama, soy sauce, pepper, dried shrimp and 200ml/7fl oz/scant 1 cup water. Cook over a medium heat for 20 minutes, or until almost dry – the jicama should be soft but not mushy. Drain off the excess juices if necessary. Leave to cool.
3 Put the wheat starch or rice flour in a large non-stick pan with 25g/1oz/¼ cup cornflour and gradually stir in the boiling water. Stir over low heat until the dough is smooth, then remove from the heat. Add the remaining cornflour and the oil. Work the dough until it is slightly elastic and moist, adding more water, if necessary.
4 When cool enough to handle, transfer the dough to a floured board and knead well, punching the dough as you work. Shape the dough into a long roll about 5cm/2in in diameter. Divide into ten pieces about 2.5cm/1in thick and flatten each with a rolling pin until about 5mm/¼in thick. Place 15ml/1 tbsp filling slightly off-centre on each dough circle. Fold over the dough to make a half-moon shape and moisten the edges. Pinch to seal the edges and trim off the excess dough.
5 Crimp the edges with a fork, then place on a lightly oiled plate and steam over simmering water for 30 minutes. Serve warm with soy sauce.

**COOK'S TIP**
It's important that the filling is quite dry, as too much moisture can cause the dough skin to burst.

Per portion Energy 307kcal/1283kJ; Protein 2.5g; Carbohydrate 40g, of which sugars 2.5g; Fat 15g, of which saturates 2.5g; Cholesterol 12.5mg; Calcium 48mg; Fibre 2g; Sodium 568mg.

# Jicama and Prawn Dumplings

This recipe is similar to the Jicama Dumplings on page 18, but in this eastern Chinese dish, Jicama is combined with fresh prawns. Jicama is not common outside of China, but they are sold fresh by some Chinese and Thai stores. Each dumpling should about 7.5cm/3in long, and half as wide.

## SERVES 4

60g/2¼oz/generous ½ cup wheat starch, plus extra for dusting
75g/3oz/⅔ cup cornflour (cornstarch)
a pinch of salt
200ml/7fl oz/scant 1 cup hot water
15ml/1 tbsp vegetable oil
sweet soy sauce (kicap manis), to serve

### For the filling

450g/1lb jicama, peeled
30ml/2 tbsp vegetable oil
2 garlic cloves, crushed
15ml/1 tbsp yellow bean sauce
5ml/1 tsp sugar
15ml/1 tbsp light soy sauce
15ml/1 tbsp sesame oil
150g/5oz small prawns (shrimp), peeled and chopped

### VARIATION
Use sliced canned bamboo shoots instead of the jicama, but cook for only 15 minutes.

1   To make the filling, cut the jicama into matchsticks about 5mm/¼in thick. Heat the oil and fry the garlic for 20 seconds, then add the yellow bean sauce, sugar, soy sauce and sesame oil. Stir for 30 seconds and then add the jicama and 500ml/17fl oz/2¼ cups water.

2   Simmer over medium heat for 25 minutes, or until nearly dry and the turnip pieces have broken up. Add the prawns and cook for 2 minutes. Allow to cool.

3   Mix the wheat starch, cornflour and salt together in a bowl and slowly add the hot water, stirring well to mix and form a soft dough. Add the oil and continue to knead a little until the mixture is the consistency of bread dough.

4   Roll out the dough into a cylinder shape on a board sprinkled with wheat starch. Cut into 12 equal pieces and form into sausage shapes. With a small rolling pin, flatten each piece into a round and roll out to 9cm/3½in in diameter.

5   Drain the jicama mixture well. Put 15ml/1 tbsp of the mixture in the centre of each piece of dough. Fold in half to make a half-moon shape. Seal the edge with a little dab of water, and crimp. Trim off any floppy edges.

6   Arrange the dumplings on a lightly oiled plate that will fit into your steamer and steam over boiling water for 15 minutes on high heat. The dumplings will have a translucent and glossy appearance. Serve with a sweet soy sauce dip.

Per portion Energy 325kcal/1363kJ; Protein 7.5g; Carbohydrate 40g, of which sugars 7.5g; Fat 15g, of which saturates 2.5g; Cholesterol 72mg; Calcium 93g; Fibre 2.5g; Sodium 468mg.

# Chive Dumplings

These dumplings are lovely and light, thanks to the wheat starch flour used for the wrappers. Although there is an art to making them, the end result is well worth the effort. The Chinese chives used in this recipe are flatter and broader than regular chives, with a distinctive, fresh aroma.

**SERVES 6–8**

150g/5oz/1¼ cups wheat starch
200ml/7fl oz/scant 1 cup water
15ml/1 tbsp vegetable oil
50g/2oz/½ cup tapioca flour
a pinch of salt
sesame oil, for brushing
chilli sauce, for dipping

**For the filling**

200g/7oz Chinese chives
30ml/2 tbsp light soy sauce
15ml/1 tbsp sesame oil
2.5ml/½ tsp ground black pepper
15ml/1 tbsp cornflour (cornstarch)
1 egg, lightly beaten

**COOK'S TIP**

Wheat starch has a very fine consistency, similar to that of cornflour (cornstarch), which you can use if you can't find wheat starch, but it is especially good for making dim sum dough. It is widely available in Chinese stores.

1   Put the wheat starch in a non-stick pan. Add the water and oil and cook over low heat, stirring occasionally, until very thick. Remove from the heat and leave to cool for 15 minutes.

2   Meanwhile, prepare the filling. Chop the chives finely, then put them in a bowl and stir in the soy sauce, sesame oil, pepper and cornflour. Heat a wok, add the mixture and toss over low heat for 5 minutes. Stir in the lightly beaten egg to bind the mixture, then set it aside.

3   Stir the tapioca flour and salt into the cooled wheat starch mixture. Mix well, then transfer to a floured board. Knead for at least 5 minutes, until the mixture is smooth and slightly elastic. Roll out the dough and stamp out 12 circles, 7.5cm/3in in diameter.

4   Place 15ml/1 tbsp of the filling on each dough circle and fold to make half-moon shapes. Seal the edges with a little water. Brush each dumpling with a little sesame oil, to prevent them from sticking together while they are being steamed.

5   Place the dumplings on a plate that will fit in your steamer, and steam over rapidly boiling water for 10 minutes, until the dumplings are glossy and translucent. Serve immediately, with a chilli sauce dip.

Per portion Energy 140kcal/589kJ; Protein 1.8g; Carbohydrate 25.9g, of which sugars 0.9g; Fat 3.9g, of which saturates 0.6g; Cholesterol 24mg; Calcium 58mg; Fibre 1.3g; Sodium 295mg.

# Sesame-coated Chicken

The use of aromatic sesame seeds is common all over China. They are sprinkled on stir-fries, ground into a cream or, as here, are used to coat pieces of meat or chicken for deep-frying. They have a delicate, nutty fragrance. Sesame seeds brown very quickly, so do not have your oil too hot.

## SERVES 4

2 skinless chicken breasts
15ml/1 tbsp sesame oil
15ml/1 tbsp light soy sauce
1 egg
25g/1oz/¼ cup sesame seeds
vegetable oil, for deep-frying

**For the vinegar and garlic dip**
4 garlic cloves, crushed
60ml/4 tbsp black or rice vinegar
a pinch of salt

1  To make the dip, mix the crushed garlic with the black or rice vinegar in a small serving bowl, and add the salt. Set aside.

2  Carefully slice through each chicken breast horizontally to make about eight thin escalopes in total (you should get four slices of chicken from each breast).

3  Place the chicken slices between sheets of clear film (plastic wrap) and tenderize them lightly by beating with a rolling pin. Season with sesame oil and soy sauce.

4  Crack the egg into a shallow dish, and beat well. Spread the sesame seeds on to a plate.

5  Coat each slice of chicken liberally with egg, then make a tight roll and roll it in the sesame seeds to coat evenly. Pat the seeds to help them stay firmly in place.

6  Heat the vegetable oil for deep-frying until a cube of bread, added to the oil, browns in about 45 seconds. Deep-fry the chicken rolls, in batches, over medium heat until golden brown and cooked through.

7  Drain on kitchen paper, and keep warm until all the chicken rolls are cooked. Serve immediately with the vinegar and garlic dip.

## VARIATION
You can also use minced (ground) chicken or pork. Shape into small balls and coat in sesame seeds before frying.

Per portion Energy 168kcal/701kJ; Protein 19g; Carbohydrate 1g, of which sugars 0g; Fat 10g, of which saturates 2g; Cholesterol 102mg; Calcium 56mg; Fibre 1g; Sodium 259mg.

# Mushrooms with Beancurd Skins

The shiitake mushrooms used in this recipe, known as black mushrooms, are the premium variety with large fissures in their caps. These are called 'winter mushrooms' in Fujian Province, and are eaten for their symbolism of longevity as well as for their rich, husky flavour and meaty texture.

## SERVES 4

16 dried shiitake mushrooms
15ml/1 tbsp dark soy sauce
5ml/1 tsp garlic paste
5ml/1 tsp ginger paste
2.5ml/½ tsp salt
2.5ml/½ tsp ground white pepper
2.5ml/½ tsp sugar
5ml/1 tsp cornflour (cornstarch)
1 or 2 sheets of beancurd skin
   (see Cook's Tip, page 28)
chilli and garlic sauce, to serve

### COOK'S TIP
These beancurd skin parcels are sometimes brushed with a little lightly thickened stock after steaming, to give them a glossy, juicy finish. They can also be deep-fried, if they are first sealed with a cornflour and water paste. Beancurd skin crisps up almost immediately in hot oil.

1   Place the shiitake mushrooms in a bowl and cover with hot water. Leave to soak for 1 hour, until soft.

2   Drain the mushrooms, snip off and discard the stems, then slice the caps as thinly as you can. Marinate the mushroom slices with the soy sauce, garlic, ginger, salt, pepper, sugar and cornflour for 10 minutes.

3   Lay a sheet of beancurd skin on a flat surface and wipe over gently with a damp cloth (this is to prevent it from cracking and splitting). Cut into pieces 13cm/5in square.

4   Put 15ml/1 tbsp of mushroom mixture on the edge of each square and roll up like a spring roll, tucking in the sides to seal as you go.

5   Put the rolls on a flat plate that will fit inside your steamer, and steam over boiling water for 10–15 minutes, topping up the water if necessary during cooking.

6   Serve the rolls immediately with a chilli and garlic sauce.

Per portion Energy 33kcal/140kJ; Protein 3g; Carbohydrate 3g, of which sugars 1g; Fat 1g, of which saturates 0g; Cholesterol 0mg; Calcium 70g; Fibre 2g; Sodium 252mg.

# Braised Beancurd Skin Parcels

Beancurd skins are a healthier option than wheat-flour-based spring roll wrappers and taste much better, especially when they have a delicious chicken, mushroom and bean sauce filling. These little parcels do not take long to steam, and make an excellent addition to a selection of dim sum.

## SERVES 4

4 dried Chinese black mushrooms
300g/11oz chicken breast
30ml/2 tbsp vegetable oil
30ml/2 tbsp black bean sauce
2.5ml/½ tsp ground black pepper
2.5ml/½ tsp sugar
30ml/2 tbsp sesame oil
100ml/3½fl oz/scant ½ cup water
1–2 sheets of beancurd skins

### COOK'S TIPS
• Dried beancurd skins are usually sold in large sheets. Check that they are not brittle or cracked, which would suggest they had been sitting too long on the grocer's shelf. Good beancurd skins should be soft and pliable.
• If the beancurd skins are a little brittle, place a damp dish towel over them for 5 minutes.
• Any unused skins should be packed flat in plastic bags, and sealed tightly. Do not refrigerate.

1  Soak the mushrooms in a bowl of boiling water for 20–30 minutes, until soft. Drain and slice into thin strips, discarding the stems. Slice the chicken into 1cm/½in thick strips.

2  Heat the vegetable oil in a wok or frying pan. Add the chicken and mushroom strips and stir-fry for 3 minutes. Add the black bean sauce, pepper, sugar and sesame oil and stir-fry for 2 minutes more.

3  Pour in the water. Cook over high heat until most of it has been driven off and the mixture is thick and almost dry. Transfer to a bowl and leave to cool.

4  Place a beancurd skin on a clean, flat surface or chopping board and cut into pieces about 10cm/4in wide. Top with two or three pieces each of chicken and mushroom, tuck in the edges and roll up to make a parcel about 6cm/2½in long. Fill the other skins in the same way.

5  Place the beancurd skin parcels on a large plate and steam over a wok of rapidly boiling water for 10 minutes. Serve hot.

Per portion Energy 188kcal/785kJ; Protein 18.6g; Carbohydrate 1.9g, of which sugars 0.6g; Fat 11.9g, of which saturates 1.7g; Cholesterol 53mg; Calcium 7mg; Fibre 0.2g; Sodium 46mg.

# Prawn and Crab Wontons

Wontons are a Cantonese invention but, over time, they have become ubiquitous throughout China, containing different fillings. These dumplings are very easy to make and lend themselves to deep-frying, steaming or adding to soups.

**SERVES 4**

250g/9oz prawns (shrimp),
  shells removed
250g/9oz white crab meat
115g/4oz tofu, finely mashed
1 egg, lightly beaten
30ml/2 tbsp light soy sauce
15ml/1 tbsp sesame oil
2.5ml/½ tsp ground black pepper
5ml/1 tsp cornflour (cornstarch)
16 wonton wrappers
vegetable oil, for deep-frying
  (optional)
chilli sauce, to serve

1  Wash and devein the prawns (*see* Cook's Tip, page 36), then mince or grind them very finely – you can do this using a mortar and pestle, or with a sharp knife. Mix with the crab meat and mashed tofu, then add the beaten egg, and mix with a wooden spoon until well combined.

2  Add the soy sauce, sesame oil, black pepper and cornflour. Stir again, and divide the mixture into 16 equal portions – each will be about a teaspoonful of mixture.

3  Using a clean finger to transfer the mixture from a teaspoon, place one portion on to a wonton wrapper. Fold the wonton wrapper up into a half-moon shape, sealing the edge with a little water. (If the wonton wrappers are square, fold them into triangles.)

4  Repeat with the other wonton wrappers. It is important to work quickly when using wonton wrappers – after making the wontons, do not let them stand for too long before cooking, as they can become brittle when exposed to the air.

5  To deep-fry the wontons, heat the oil in a wok or deep-fryer to 190°C/375°F, add the wontons, and cook until golden brown. Alternatively, steam them over a pan of boiling water for 10 minutes, until the prawn mixture is cooked through. Serve with a chilli sauce dip.

### VARIATION
Tofu is added here, but you can also use the same amount of minced (ground) pork instead, if you prefer.

Per portion Energy 451kcal/874kJ; Protein 30g; Carbohydrate 13g, of which sugars 1g; Fat 31g, of which saturates 4g; Cholesterol 225mg; Calcium 207mg; Fibre 1g; Sodium 762mg.

# Butterfly Prawns

A classic Cantonese restaurant dish, this takes its name from the way each prawn is slit and opened out so that it looks like a butterfly. The prawns are dipped in a very light batter, almost like tempura, and then quickly cooked in very hot oil until golden and crispy.

## SERVES 4

16 large prawns (shrimp)
30ml/2 tbsp plain
   (all-purpose) flour
15ml/1 tbsp self-raising
   (self-rising) flour
a pinch of bicarbonate of soda
   (baking soda)
15ml/1 tbsp sesame oil
120ml/4fl oz/½ cup cold water
vegetable oil, for deep-frying
chilli and garlic dipping sauce,
   to serve

1   Clean the prawns and remove the shells, but leave the tails intact. Using a sharp knife, slit each prawn halfway through the back. Devein the prawns by removing the black vein using a toothpick (cocktail stick), then spread them flat so that they resemble butterflies.

2   Mix the plain flour and self-raising flour in a bowl. Add the bicarbonate of soda, then the sesame oil and cold water. Stir to make a smooth batter.

3   Heat the oil in a wok or deep-fryer to 190°C/375°F. Dip each prawn in turn in the batter, gently shaking off the excess, and add to the hot oil. Repeat with more prawns, but do not overcrowd the wok or fryer (it is best to work in batches).

4   After 2–3 minutes, when the prawns are golden brown and cooked through, lift them out using a slotted spoon, and drain on kitchen paper. Keep warm while cooking successive batches. Serve hot, with the chilli and garlic dipping sauce.

### COOK'S TIPS
• For a crisp batter, always use very cold water or iced water.
• If you do not have time to butterfly the prawns, simply shell them, dip them in batter and fry as above. They will not looks as good but will still taste delicious.
• Serve the prawns immediately after frying, when the batter is still very hot.

Per portion Energy 156kcal/653kJ; Protein 12.5g; Carbohydrate 7.3g, of which sugars 0.5g; Fat 8.8g, of which saturates 1.3g; Cholesterol 157mg; Calcium 64mg; Fibre 0.3g; Sodium 316mg.

# Paper-wrapped Prawns

The paper used for these prawn parcels is completely edible. Sold as 'wafer pastry' in Chinese supermarkets, it is extremely delicate and needs deft handling. The prawns are seasoned with lime juice and oyster sauce then wrapped in the pastry and immediately fried until crisp and light.

**SERVES 4**

16 tiger prawns (jumbo
   shrimp), peeled
15ml/1 tbsp oyster sauce
5ml/1 tsp lime juice
5ml/1 tsp caster (superfine) sugar
5ml/1 tsp ground black pepper
15ml/1 tbsp cornflour (cornstarch)
vegetable oil, for deep-frying
30ml/2 tbsp sesame oil
16 or more Chinese wafer
   pastry sheets

**For the chilli dip**
3–4 red chillies, finely chopped
60–75ml/4–5 tbsp Kao Liang
   vinegar
a pinch of salt

## VARIATION
Instead of the pastry wrappers, coat the prawns liberally with cornflour or tapioca flour and then drop them into the hot oil. They will have a thin, crisp coating.

1   Make a shallow cut down the centre of the curved back of each prawn. Pull out the black vein with a cocktail stick (toothpick) or your fingers, then rinse the prawn thoroughly and pat dry. Make a deep slit down the underside to open up the prawns and give them a better shape. Put them in a shallow dish.

2   Put the oyster sauce in a small bowl and mix in the lime juice, sugar, pepper and cornflour. Sprinkle this seasoning over the prawns and turn to coat.

3   To make the chilli dip, grind the chillies in a mortar and pestle until very fine. Add the vinegar and salt, and stir to mix.

4   Heat the vegetable oil in a wok or deep-fryer to 190°C/375°F, then add the sesame oil. Remove a pastry sheet carefully and place a prawn in the middle. Fold the pastry up, drawing all sides toward the centre, and press the edges together to seal in the prawn. If the moistness of the marinade renders the pastry a little mushy, wrap both the prawn and the paper in an additional paper.

5   Drop the parcel into the oil. Remove with a slotted spoon as soon as it turns light brown. The pastry will firm up as it browns in the hot oil; be careful not to let it scorch. Wrap and cook the remaining prawn parcels as you make them; do not pre-wrap the prawns and leave them to fry in one go, as they will quickly become soggy. Drain on kitchen paper and serve with the chilli dip.

Per portion Energy 288kcal/1214kJ; Protein 10g; Carbohydrate 18g, of which sugars 2g; Fat 20g, of which saturates 3g; Cholesterol 98mg; Calcium 46mg; Fibre 0 g; Sodium 563mg.

# Fried Prawn Balls

Fujian chefs are very good at processing shellfish and fish into savoury balls and cakes, such as these prawn balls. Although the mixture needs a bit of work to achieve the correct consistency, the resulting balls are superior to commercial ones, which tend to contain a lot of flour.

## SERVES 4

675g/1½lb prawns (shrimp),
  peeled and deveined
  (see Cook's Tip)
30ml/2 tbsp water
30ml/2 tbsp tapioca starch or
  cornflour (cornstarch), plus extra
  for dusting
5ml/1 tsp salt
15ml/1 tbsp sesame oil
2.5ml/½ tsp ground white pepper
25g/1oz cloud ear (wood ear)
  mushrooms, soaked in cold
  water for 20 minutes
vegetable oil, for deep-frying
chilli sauce, for dipping

### COOK'S TIP
To devein a prawn, make a shallow cut down the centre of the curved back of the prawn. Pull out the black vein with a cocktail stick (toothpick) or your fingers. Rinse the prawn well.

1  Process the prawns to a smooth paste in a blender or food processor. Transfer to a mortar and grind slowly with a pestle. As you do this, add the water and tapioca starch or cornflour a little at a time, turning the prawn paste as you work.

2  Add the salt, sesame oil and pepper, and blend well using the pestle. Continue to process the prawns in this way for at least 15 minutes. This will aerate the prawn mixture until it has a slightly springy texture. Alternatively, use a food processor or blender, although the results will not be quite the same, because of the cutting action of the blade rather than the grinding action of the pestle.

3  Using scissors, trim off and discard any hard woody parts from the cloud ears, then chop them finely. Add to the prawns and continue to process until well mixed.

4  With floured fingers, shape the mixture into small balls the size of large grapes. Heat the oil for deep-frying in a wok or deep-fryer to 190°C/375°F. Deep-fry the prawn balls until golden brown, then remove and leave to cool. The balls will shrink a little, with slightly shrivelled skin; this is normal. Serve with chilli sauce for dipping.

Per portion Energy 252kcal/1054kJ; Protein 30g; Carbohydrate 11g, of which sugars 0g; Fat 10g, of which saturates 1g; Cholesterol 329mg; Calcium 139g; Fibre 0g; Sodium 815mg.

# Prawn Cutlets

In the inland areas of northern China, fishermen sell delicious fresh prawns from their small boats on the riverbanks, immediately after catching them. Most of us are not able to buy prawns direct from a fishing boat, but do try to buy the freshest ones you can, as this will provide the best flavour.

## SERVES 4

450g/1lb prawns (shrimp), peeled and deveined (see Cook's Tip, page 36)
200g/7oz firm tofu
15ml/1 tbsp sesame oil
15ml/1 tbsp light soy sauce
5ml/1 tsp ground black pepper
2 eggs
45ml/3 tbsp cornflour (cornstarch)
vegetable oil, for deep-frying

**For the accompaniments**
English (hot) or Dijon mustard
chilli sauce
black vinegar
1 cucumber, sliced into thin rounds
75g/3oz pickled ginger

1   Place all the dips and accompaniments into individual dipping bowls, and set aside.

2   Mince (grind) the prawns until fine – you can do this using a mortar and pestle, or with a sharp knife.

3   Mash the tofu with a fork until smooth, then mix with the prawns. Add the sesame oil, soy sauce and pepper, and blend well.

4   Beat the eggs lightly and add to the mixture. Stir well to combine. Shape into four patties, each about 6cm/2½in in diameter and 1cm/½in thick.

5   Heat the oil for deep-frying in a wok or deep-fryer to 190°C/375°F. Coat the patties with cornflour, and deep-fry them until golden brown and cooked through. Serve immediately, with the dips and accompaniments.

## VARIATION
The same weight of mashed potato can be used as a binding agent instead of tofu.

Per portion Energy 332kcal/1386kJ; Protein 28g; Carbohydrate 11g, of which sugars 0g; Fat 20g, of which saturates 3g; Cholesterol 335mg; Calcium 365mg; Fibre 0g; Sodium 443mg.

# Steamed Prawn Dumplings

These dumplings uses wheat starch (known as mien fen in Mandarin), mixed with cornflour to achieve a translucent pasty. The dough dries out quickly, so it needs to be filled and cooked immediately.

## SERVES 4

60g/2¼oz/generous ½ cup wheat
　starch, plus extra for dusting
75g/3oz/⅔ cup cornflour
　(cornstarch)
a pinch of salt
200ml/7fl oz/1 cup hot water
soy sauce or chilli sauce,
　to serve

### For the filling

675g/1½lb prawns (shrimp)
5ml/1 tsp sugar
5ml/1 tsp cornflour (cornstarch)
1 spring onion (scallion),
　finely chopped
5ml/1 tsp salt
2.5ml/½ tsp sugar
2.5ml/½ tsp ground white pepper

### COOK'S TIP
Wheat starch has a fine
consistency, similar to that of
cornflour (cornstarch). It is
especially good for making
dim sum dough and is widely
available in Chinese stores.

1　To make the filling, peel, wash and devein the prawns, and cut each into small dice. Mix the sugar and cornflour in a bowl and rub the prawn pieces gently in the mixture to coat thoroughly. Wash off the cornflour and sugar by putting the prawns in a colander and rinsing them under running water for 10 minutes. Drain well. This gives the prawns a delicious crunch.

2　In a bowl, combine the prawn pieces, spring onion, salt, sugar and pepper. Put into a pan and cook over a low heat for 5 minutes, stirring often, or until the prawns turn pink with a fairly thick coating. Allow to cool.

3　In a bowl, mix the wheat starch, cornflour and salt together, then slowly add the hot water, mixing well to form a soft dough. The consistency should be similar to bread dough, but less springy.

4　Roll the dough into a cylinder shape on a board sprinkled with wheat starch flour. Cut into 20 equal pieces and form into balls. With a small rolling pin, flatten each piece into a round and roll out until about 7.5cm/3in in diameter.

5　Put one heaped teaspoonful of prawn mixture into the centre of a piece of dough. Fold in half to make a half-moon shape. Pinch the ends together, then pleat and shape into a closed dumpling. Repeat with the other dough pieces.

6　Arrange the dumplings on a lightly oiled plate. Steam over a pan of boiling water for 15 minutes on high heat. Serve with a soy sauce or chilli sauce dip.

Per dumpling Energy 260kcal/1105kJ; Protein 30g; Carbohydrate 35g, of which sugars 0g; Fat 0g, of which saturates 0g; Cholesterol 330mg; Calcium 145g: Fibre 0g; Sodium 830mg.

# Little Dragon Dumplings

Within the dim sum menu, these dumplings, called xiao long bau in Mandarin, are among the most popular. How their name came about remains a mystery, but the dragon reigns supreme in Chinese culture. High-gluten flour is necessary for making the dough; it is available in most Chinese stores.

SERVES 4

200g/7oz high gluten flour (gou garn fun), plus extra for dusting
75g/3oz/⅔ cup plain (all-purpose) flour
200ml/7fl oz/scant 1 cup boiling water
30ml/2 tbsp vegetable oil, lard or white cooking fat
chilli sauce or soy sauce, to serve

**For the filling**
200g/7oz prawns (shrimp)
200g/7oz/1¾ cups minced (ground) pork
5ml/1 tsp cornflour (cornstarch)
15ml/1 tbsp chopped Chinese celery
3 spring onions (scallions), chopped
30ml/2 tbsp light soy sauce
30ml/2 tbsp sesame oil
2.5ml/½ tsp ground black pepper
a pinch of sugar

1 To make the filling, first roughly mince (grind) the prawns using a pestle and mortar or a sharp knife, then combine them with the minced pork and cornflour.
2 Add 60ml/4 tbsp water, the Chinese celery, spring onions, soy sauce, sesame oil, pepper and sugar. Stir well, then set aside.
3 Mix the flours in a bowl and pour over the boiling water. Add the oil or fat, and stir with a wooden spoon. As soon as the mixture is cool enough to handle, knead it on a floured work surface for 5 minutes. You may find the dough rather crumbly, but keep scooping up the floury parts and kneading them into the dough.
4 Continue to knead until the dough is smooth and elastic (like bread dough). Roll out into a long sausage shape, 2cm/¾in in diameter. Cut it into 12 pieces and shape into small balls.
5 With a rolling pin, flatten each piece until paper-thin. The dough is very elastic, and will not break. Put a heaped teaspoonful of filling on to each 'skin' and wrap it into a half-moon shape.
6 Seal and crimp the edges; shape each dumpling so that the crimped edge is lying across the top of the dumpling. Place the dumplings on a lightly oiled plate that will fit into your steamer, and steam for 15 minutes, or until the skins become slightly translucent. Serve warm with a chilli sauce or soy sauce dip.

Per portion Energy 482kcal/2027kJ; Protein 28g; Carbohydrate 55g, of which sugars 1g; Fat18g, of which saturates 3g; Cholesterol 129mg; Calcium 145mg; Fibre 3g; Sodium 493mg.

# Pork and Prawn Dumplings

While dim sum are generally attributed to southern China, these bitesize morsels, called shao mai, are enjoyed throughout the entire country. Pork is the main ingredient in the filling used here, but there are also versions that contain just prawns or seafood.

### SERVES 4

100g/3¾oz prawns (shrimp),
  peeled and deveined (see
  Cook's Tip, page 36)
2 spring onions (scallions)
225g/8oz/1 cup minced
  (ground) pork
30ml/2 tbsp light soy sauce
15ml/1 tbsp sesame oil
2.5ml/½ tsp ground black pepper
15ml/1 tbsp cornflour (cornstarch)
16 round wonton wrappers
16 large garden peas,
  thawed if frozen
chilli sauce, for dipping

1  Chop the prawns finely to make a coarse paste. This can be done using a sharp knife or in a food processor, but if you use a food processor use the pulse button, or the prawns will become rubbery. Scrape into a bowl.

2  Chop the spring onions very finely. Add them to the puréed prawns, with the minced pork, soy sauce, sesame oil, ground black pepper and cornflour. Mix well.

3  Holding a wonton wrapper on the palm of one hand, spoon a heaped teaspoon of the filling into the centre. Cup your hand so that the wrapper enfolds the filling to make the classic dumpling shape. Leave the top slightly open. Top each gap with a pea. Fill the remaining wonton wrappers in the same way, working quickly so the wrappers do not dry out.

4  Place the dumplings on a lightly oiled plate and steam over a wok of rapidly boiling water for 10 minutes, until the prawn mixture is cooked through. Serve with a chilli sauce dip.

### COOK'S TIP
If you can only find square wonton wrappers, trim off the corners to make a rough circle before filling them.

Per portion Energy 228kcal/957kJ; Protein 18.2g; Carbohydrate 20.2g, of which sugars 1.3g; Fat 8.8g, of which saturates 2.5g; Cholesterol 86mg; Calcium 57mg; Fibre 1.3g; Sodium 622mg.

# Roast Pork Dumplings

Known as char siew bau in Cantonese, these quintessential dim sum delicacies owe their excellence to a trade secret that has long eluded the common cook. The secret lies in the special low gluten flour that makes these dumplings light, white and fluffy. It is available in Chinese food stores.

## SERVES 4

200g/7oz/1¾ cups low gluten
   flour (dai garn fun)
pinch of salt
5ml/1 tsp easy bake (rapid-rise)
   dried yeast
120ml/4fl oz/½ cup warm water
5ml/1 tsp vinegar
soy sauce, for dipping

### For the filling

115g/4oz cold roast pork,
   finely diced
30ml/2 tbsp hoisin sauce
1 spring onion (scallion),
   finely chopped

### COOK'S TIP
Don't throw away the bits of pastry you pinch off the top of the dumplings. Rolled together, they will yield enough dough for two more dumplings.

1 Put the flour and salt in a large mixing bowl and sprinkle in the yeast. Make a well in the centre and pour in the warm water and vinegar. Mix to a dough.

2 Place the dough on a floured board and knead for 10 minutes. Return it to the bowl, cover and set aside to rise for 20 minutes or until doubled in bulk.

3 Knock back (punch down) the dough, knead it again, return it to the bowl and set aside in a warm place for 15 minutes.

4 Meanwhile, make the filling. Put the diced pork in a bowl. Stir in the hoisin sauce to moisten it, then add the spring onion.

5 Roll out the dough on a floured board and shape it into a 30cm/12in long roll, about 5cm/2in in diameter. Cut the roll into 2.5cm/1in slices and flatten each with a rolling pin to a thin round, about 9cm/3½in across.

6 Holding a pastry round on the palm of one hand, add a heaped teaspoonful of the filling to the centre. Cup your hand so that the dough enfolds the filling, pleating and pinching it where necessary. Pinch off the excess dough at the top and seal with a twisting action. Fill the remaining dumplings in the same way.

7 Cut 12 pieces of baking parchment, 5cm/2in square. Stand a dumpling on each piece of paper in a steamer. Steam over a wok of boiling water for 15 minutes, until cooked through. Serve immediately, with soy sauce for dipping.

Per portion Energy 219kcal/927kJ; Protein 7.2g; Carbohydrate 46.8g, of which sugars 0.6g; Fat 1.5g, of which saturates 0.6g; Cholesterol 18mg; Calcium 12mg; Fibre 0g; Sodium 582mg.

# Pork and Nut Dumplings

These dainty little bites use basically the same dough as for chive dumplings, but their taste and texture is totally different. This is thanks to the unusual filling, with its interplay of succulent pork, crunchy nuts and aromatics. These are a typical Shantou dim sum.

**SERVES 6–8**

150g/5oz/1¼ cups wheat starch
200ml/7fl oz/scant 1 cup water
15ml/1 tbsp vegetable oil
50g/2oz/½ cup tapioca flour or
 cornflour (cornstarch)
a pinch of salt

### For the filling

30ml/2 tbsp vegetable oil
200g/7oz/scant 1 cup minced
 (ground) pork
90ml/6 tbsp water
50g/2oz/½ cup peanuts, chopped
30ml/2 tbsp light soy sauce
15ml/1 tbsp sesame oil
2.5ml/½ tsp black pepper

### For the black vinegar and
### ginger dip

45ml/3 tbsp black vinegar
5ml/1 tbsp finely grated
 (shredded) fresh root ginger
a small pinch of salt

1 Put the wheat starch in a non-stick pan. Add the water and oil and cook over low heat, stirring occasionally, until very thick. Remove from the heat and leave to cool for 15 minutes.

2 Meanwhile, make the filling. Heat the oil in a small pan and fry the pork for 2 minutes. Add the water, chopped peanuts, soy sauce, sesame oil and ground black pepper. Stir for 3 minutes until the pork is cooked through and there is the barest hint of sauce. Set aside to cool.

3 Stir the tapioca flour and salt into the cool wheat starch mixture. Mix well, then transfer to a floured board. Knead for at least 5 minutes. Divide into 12 portions. Flatten each piece of dough and roll them into 7.5cm/3in circles.

4 Place a heaped tablespoonful of the filling on each dough circle and fold to make half-moon shapes. Seal the edges with a little water. Brush each dumpling with a little sesame oil to prevent them from sticking together during steaming.

5 Place the dumplings on a large plate and steam over a wok of rapidly boiling water for 10 minutes.

6 Meanwhile, mix together all the ingredients for the black vinegar and ginger dip in a small bowl. Transfer to a serving bowl. Serve the dumplings hot, with the dipping sauce.

Per portion Energy 216kcal/906kJ; Protein 6.7g; Carbohydrate 24.3g, of which sugars 0.7g; Fat 10.9g, of which saturates 2.1g; Cholesterol 17mg; Calcium 10mg; Fibre 0.4g; Sodium 294mg.

# Pork and Cabbage Dumplings

These dumplings are Hubei staples that are eaten as snacks. Unlike Western dumplings, they are usually made with self-raising flour and dry yeast. The filling is a mild blend of fried minced pork and cabbage flavoured with pepper, garlic and soy sauce.

**SERVES 4**

200g/7oz/1¾ cups self-raising (self-rising) flour, plus extra for dusting
15g/½oz/1 tbsp easy bake (rapid-rise) yeast
a pinch of salt
5ml/1 tsp caster (superfine) sugar
120ml/4fl oz/½ cup warm water

**For the filling**

75g/3oz white cabbage leaves
30ml/2 tbsp groundnut (peanut) oil
2 garlic cloves, crushed
90g/3½oz/scant ½ cup minced (ground) pork
30ml/2 tbsp dark soy sauce
2.5ml/½ tsp ground black pepper
2.5ml/½ tsp caster (superfine) sugar
1.5ml/¼ tsp salt

### VARIATION

For a richer flavour, halve the amount of soy sauce and add 15ml/1 tbsp oyster sauce.

1  Sift the flour into a large bowl and stir in the yeast, salt and sugar. Make a well in the centre and pour in the warm water. Stir the water into the dry ingredients to form a slightly sticky dough, then knead for 10 minutes on a floured surface. Return to the bowl, cover with a damp dish towel, and leave in a warm place to rise for 30–40 minutes, or until doubled in bulk.

2  Gently turn the dough over to deflate it, then cover and leave for a further 15 minutes. Meanwhile, make the filling. Fill a pan with boiling water and plunge in the cabbage leaves for 45 seconds–1 minute, or until just limp. Drain thoroughly in a colander, then squeeze the leaves to remove the excess moisture. Finely chop the cabbage.

3  Heat the oil in a wok or pan over a high heat and fry the garlic for 30 seconds. Add the minced pork and chopped cabbage, and fry for 1 minute. Add the soy sauce, pepper, sugar, salt and 100ml/3½fl oz/scant ½ cup water, then cook for 3 minutes, or until nearly dry. Spread the filling on to a plate to cool completely.

4  Press out the dough into a rectangle on a floured surface. Roll it up tightly into a log about 5cm/2in in diameter, then cut into 12 slices. Dust a slice with flour and, with a small rolling pin, roll it out into a round 9cm/3½in in diameter, making the edges slightly thinner than the centre.

5  Place a heaped teaspoonful of filling in the centre of the round and bring up the sides to enclose the filling, ruching and gathering up the edge as you rotate the dumpling in your palm. Pinch the gathered-up top tightly to seal, and pinch off the excess dough, leaving a neat little button. Make the remaining dumplings in the same way.

6  Cut 12 5cm/2in squares of baking parchment. Place each dumpling on a parchment square, then transfer to a steamer over simmering water. Steam over a high heat for 15 minutes.

Per portion Energy 285kcal/1203kJ; Protein 12g; Carbohydrate 42g, of which sugars 3g; Fat 9g, of which saturates 3g; Cholesterol 15mg; Calcium 192mg; Fibre 2.1g; Sodium 873mg.

# Minced Pork Rolls in Beancurd Skin

This classic dish of the Swatow people from Shantou is so sublime that it is often cooked as a festive offering during Taoist festivals. It is unique in that it uses crinkly beancurd skins as wrappers. Unlike many regional Chinese dishes, this is a local dish and seldom appears on menus elsewhere.

SERVES 4

400g/14oz/1¾ cups minced
   (ground) pork
1 small carrot, thinly shredded
10ml/2 tsp light soy sauce
5ml/1 tsp ground black pepper
50g/2oz/⅓ cup finely chopped
   drained canned water chestnuts
8 spring onions (scallions),
   finely chopped
1 egg
25g/1oz/¼ cup cornflour
   (cornstarch)
1 package beancurd skins
vegetable oil for deep-frying
sliced cucumber and chilli sauce,
   to serve

1  Put the pork in a bowl and add the shredded carrot. Stir in the soy sauce, black pepper, water chestnuts and spring onions.

2  Lightly beat the egg in a small bowl and add it to the mixture. Stir to combine, then add the cornflour and mix well.

3  Bring a small pan of water to the boil. Pinch off a small lump of the pork mixture, add it to the water and boil for 2 minutes. Scoop it out, let it cool slightly, then taste and adjust the seasoning if necessary.

4  Keeping the remaining beancurd sheets covered under a damp dish towel, place one sheet on a flat surface. Spread about 30ml/2 tbsp of the pork mixture along one edge. Roll over one and a half times, fold in the sides, then roll again to make a firm roll. Cut through the beancurd to separate the roll from the sheet. Repeat the action, using more sheets when required, until all the filling has been used.

5  Heat the oil in a wok or deep-fryer to 190°C/375°F. Add the rolls and fry for 3–4 minutes until cooked through, golden brown and crisp. Drain on kitchen paper and leave to cool.

6  Slice diagonally into pieces, and serve with sliced cucumber and chilli sauce for dipping.

### COOK'S TIP
Beancurd skins are sometimes brittle, so wipe each sheet with a damp towel before use.

Per portion Energy 387kcal/1608kJ; Protein 23.8g; Carbohydrate 8.6g, of which sugars 2.4g; Fat 28.9g, of which saturates 6.1g; Cholesterol 114mg; Calcium 158mg; Fibre 0.9g; Sodium 361mg.

# Deep-fried Wontons

These are a close cousin of shao mai (Pork and Prawn Dumplings). They have much the same ingredients but are fried rather than steamed. Crisp on the outside, with a tender filling, these will be very popular, so it is a good idea to make double the quantity.

SERVES 4

300g/11oz/1½ cups minced (ground) pork
15ml/1 tbsp light soy sauce
15ml/1 tbsp sesame oil
2.5ml/½ tsp ground black pepper
15ml/1 tbsp cornflour (cornstarch)
16 wonton wrappers
vegetable oil for deep-frying
chilli dipping sauce or plum sauce, to serve

1   Put the minced pork in a bowl. Add the light soy sauce, sesame oil, ground black pepper and cornflour. Mix well.

2   Place about 5ml/1 tsp of the mixture in the centre of a wonton wrapper, bring the corners together so that they meet at the top, and pinch the neck to seal. Fill the remaining wontons in the same way, working quickly to avoid the wonton wrappers drying out.

3   Heat the oil in a wok or deep-fryer to 190°C/375°F. Carefully add the filled wontons, about four or five at a time, and deep-fry until golden brown and cooked through.

4   Carefully lift out the cooked wontons with a slotted spoon, drain on kitchen paper and keep hot while frying successive batches. Serve the wontons hot with chilli dipping sauce or plum sauce.

## COOK'S TIPS
• If the wonton skins are brittle, wipe them with a damp towel or they will be difficult to shape without cracking.
• Filled wontons take very little time to cook. Make sure your oil is not too hot as they scorch very quickly.

Per portion Energy 326kcal/1357kJ; Protein 16.3g; Carbohydrate 18.3g, of which sugars 0.6g; Fat 21.3g, of which saturates 4.4g; Cholesterol 50mg; Calcium 33mg; Fibre 0.6g; Sodium 319mg.

# Lotus Leaf Dumplings

Rice, fish, shellfish, meat and all manner of other ingredients are cooked, wrapped in lotus leaves and steamed in provinces all over China. The leaves are very large but can be trimmed to make more dainty parcels, each one a delicious combination of pork, lotus seeds and succulent quail's eggs.

## SERVES 4

30ml/2 tbsp vegetable oil
2 garlic cloves, crushed
200g/7oz belly pork, diced
8 Chinese mushrooms, soaked
  and chopped
16 canned lotus seeds
16 quail's eggs, hard-boiled
  and peeled
20g/¾oz chopped Chinese
  celery leaves
30ml/2 tbsp oyster sauce
30ml/2 tbsp Shaoxing wine
  or dry sherry
5ml/1 tsp ground black pepper
15ml/1 tbsp dark soy sauce
10ml/2 tsp cornflour (cornstarch)
2 lotus leaves, soaked until soft

### COOK'S TIPS
• Quail's eggs take about
  5 minutes to hard-boil.
• If the lotus leaves appear to
  be brittle, use a double layer
  for extra strength. They are
  actually quite resilient and do
  not tear easily.

1  Heat the oil in a wok and fry the garlic for 2 minutes. Add the pork and stir-fry for 3 minutes, or until sealed all over.

2  Add the mushrooms and lotus seeds, then fry for 2 minutes.

3  Add the quail's eggs, celery, oyster sauce, wine or dry sherry, pepper and soy sauce, then stir gently with a wooden spoon so that you do not to break up the delicate quail's eggs.

4  Blend the cornflour with 75ml/5 tbsp water and add to the pan. Stir until the cornflour thickens the sauce and binds all the ingredients together. Transfer the filling to a bowl and set aside.

5  Trim the lotus leaves and cut each into two fan-shaped halves. Divide the mixture between the four leaf halves (there should be about 45ml/3 tbsp on each), making sure there is a good mixture of pork, mushrooms, lotus seeds and quail's eggs in each parcel. Wrap each parcel securely, folding over the sides.

6  Steam for 15 minutes, then serve immediately – the parcels should be opened at the table.

Per portion Energy 309kcal/1289kJ; Protein 16g; Carbohydrate 10g, of which sugars 0g; Fat 22g, of which saturates 6g; Cholesterol 192mg; Calcium 39mg; Fibre 1g; Sodium 590mg.

# Quail's Egg Sesame Toast

Sesame toast is a favourite on dim sum menus and makes a good choice of finger food when entertaining. This recipe has a hard-boiled quail's egg sitting beneath the usual filling of minced pork. When coated with sesame seeds and deep-fried, these have an intriguing flavour and texture.

### SERVES 4

4 quail's eggs, hard-boiled
4 slices of white bread, crusts
  removed
2 eggs, lightly beaten
250g/9oz/generous 1 cup minced
  (ground) pork
15ml/1 tbsp light soy sauce
2.5ml/½ tsp white pepper
5ml/1 tsp cornflour (cornstarch)
sesame seeds, for coating
vegetable oil, for deep-frying
sliced cucumber and hoisin sauce
  or chilli sauce, to serve

1  Place the quail's eggs in a pan of boiling water and cook for 5 minutes. Drain then cool in cold water. Remove the shells from the eggs and cut each in half.

2  Cut each slice of bread into two triangles. Brush with beaten egg. Mix the minced pork with the soy sauce, pepper and cornflour, stirring well.

3  Place a halved quail's egg, cut side down, on each bread triangle and spread minced pork over the top, patting it in firmly. Brush with beaten egg.

4  Spread a generous amount of sesame seeds over a plate and carefully coat the top of each covered toast liberally. Shake off the excess.

5  Heat the oil to 180°C/350°F in a pan or deep-fryer, and fry the toasts (in batches) until golden brown and the pork is cooked through.

6  Serve immediately with sliced cucumber and hoisin sauce or chilli sauce, for dipping.

### VARIATION
You can also use minced (ground) chicken or prawns (shrimp), instead of pork.

Per portion Energy 342kcal/3426kJ; Protein 24g; Carbohydrate 16g, of which sugars 2g; Fat 20g, of which saturates 4g; Cholesterol 336mg; Calcium 94g; Fibre 2g; Sodium 508mg.

# Beef Cakes

Usually served at festive occasions, these make hearty snacks and can be made well in advance, then warmed up or lightly re-fried. They go very well with the vinegar, ginger and spring onion dip on page 62. The traditional recipe uses solid pork fat, but bacon rind can be used as a substitute.

**MAKES 8**

200g/7oz/1¾ cups plain
  (all-purpose) flour, plus extra
  for dusting
40g/1½oz/⅓ cup tapioca flour
a pinch of salt
200ml/7fl oz/scant 1 cup
  boiling water
15ml/1 tbsp vegetable oil, plus
  about 75ml/5 tbsp for frying

**For the filling**

200g/7oz/1¾ cups minced
  (ground) beef
75g/3oz pork fat or bacon fat,
  finely chopped
75ml/3 tbsp water
30ml/2 tbsp light soy sauce
2.5ml/½ tsp ground black pepper
2 spring onions (scallions),
  finely chopped
25g/1oz fresh root ginger, grated
a pinch of sugar
30ml/2 tbsp sesame oil
salt (optional)

1   Place all the filling ingredients in a bowl and mix together thoroughly. Pinch off a small ball, cook it quickly in a small pan, then taste to check the seasoning. Add salt to taste, if needed. Cook the rest of the mixture in the pan for about 5 minutes until the beef is cooked through, then set it aside to cool.

2   Sift the flours into a mixing bowl and add the salt. Mix well and gradually add the boiling water, stirring well. Add the 15ml/1 tbsp vegetable oil. When cool enough to handle, transfer the dough to a floured surface, and knead for 5 minutes, until smooth.

3   Roll out into a long sausage shape and cut into eight pieces. Flatten each piece into a thin circle about 9cm/3½in in diameter, or as thin as you can make them without breaking them. Divide the beef mixture between the eight circles (there should be about a heaped tablespoonful on each). Draw the sides in to the centre, then pinch to seal firmly. Smooth the sealed sides, then shape and flatten them gently into round, flat cakes with the sealed side underneath.

4   Heat a frying pan with the 75ml/5 tbsp oil and fry the cakes, in batches, for 3 minutes on each side, or until golden brown. Add more oil, if necessary, for each batch, but make sure you heat it up before adding the remaining cakes to the pan.

Per portion Energy 304kcal/1268kJ; Protein 10g; Carbohydrate 25g, of which sugars 1g; Fat 19g, of which saturates 4g; Cholesterol 20mg; Calcium 44mg; Fibre 1g; Sodium 232mg.

# Beef and Mushroom Dumplings

This is a typical steamed dim sum dish from Henan, and it is sometimes made with minced lamb. Seasonings for dumplings in northern China tend to contain wine to give a rich flavour.

**SERVES 4**

200g/7oz high gluten flour (gou garn fun), plus extra for dusting
75g/3oz/⅔ cup plain (all-purpose) flour
200ml/7fl oz/scant 1 cup boiling water
30ml/2 tbsp vegetable oil, lard or white cooking fat

**For the dip**

25g/1oz fresh root ginger
1 spring onion (scallion)
75ml/5 tbsp black vinegar
a pinch of salt

**For the filling**

400g/14oz/3½ cups minced (ground) beef
5ml/1 tsp cornflour (cornstarch)
30ml/2 tbsp oyster sauce
15ml/1 tbsp Shaoxing wine or dry sherry
2.5ml/½ tsp ground black pepper
1 spring onion (scallion), finely chopped
15ml/1 tbsp ground ginger
8 Chinese mushrooms, soaked until soft

1 To make the dip, peel and grate the ginger, and chop the spring onion very finely. Place them in a bowl with the black vinegar and salt. Mix well, then set aside.
2 To make the filling, mix the minced beef with the cornflour, oyster sauce, wine or sherry, pepper, spring onion and ginger. Chop the mushrooms finely and add to the beef mixture. Mix together well and set aside.
3 Mix the flours in a mixing bowl, and pour over the boiling water. Add the oil or fat, and stir with a wooden spoon. As soon as the mixture is cool enough to handle, transfer it to a floured work surface and knead for 5 minutes. The dough may be crumbly, but keep scooping up the floury parts and kneading them into the dough.
4 Continue to knead until the dough is smooth and elastic (it should have the consistency of bread dough). Roll out into a long sausage shape, 2cm/¾in in diameter. Cut it into 12 pieces and shape into small balls.
5 With a rolling pin, flatten each piece until it is paper-thin. It will not break, as the dough is very elastic. Put a tablespoonful of filling on to each round and fold it over into a half-moon shape. Seal and crimp the edges; shape each dumpling so that the crimped edge is lying across the top of the dumpling.
6 Place the dumplings on a lightly oiled plate that will fit into your steamer and steam over boiling water for 15 minutes, or until the skins become slightly translucent and the filling is cooked through. Serve warm with the dip.

Per portion Energy 531kcal/2298kJ; Protein 30g; Carbohydrate 63g, of which sugars 3g; Fat 18g, of which saturates 6g; Cholesterol 57mg; Calcium 126mg; Fibre 3g; Sodium 459mg.

# Index